Chasing the Moon

Book 2 of the

Mr. Nibbles' Bites of Life

Series

By Mr. Nibbles and
Leslie Goodale Adebonojo

Spring Knoll Press
2018

This book is a work of fiction. The character in this story, Mr. Nibbles, does not represent any other dog. Any resemblance to any other dog living or dead is entirely coincidental.

Copyright © 2018 by Leslie Adebonojo

All rights reserved.

Published in the United States.

Spring Knoll Press

ISBN-13: 978-0-9978746-5-5

For Geoff

You always encouraged me to do it, so, I did it again with pictures.

Love, mom

Thank you to Donna Mobley Mohon, my BFF, for the photographs of the moon.

And thank you to Katy Libby the best editor ever.

Discussions and observations you may want to have with your child.

This book has been designed to encourage children to create their own story to go along with the pictures.

Page

1 - What is an animal shelter? Why do animals live in a shelter? Why do you think the dog's name is Mr. Nibbles? (Hint: he likes to nibble on your toes and fingers, but never too hard)

3-5 - Is Mr. Nibbles playing with the moon? Does his ball look like the moon? What is the moon?

6 - Mr. Nibbles has many rubber balls to play with. In his first book he used his purple ball, in this book he has a white ball. What do you like to play with?

8-14 - Can you follow Mr. Nibbles as he searches for the Moon among the beautiful daffodils?

Daffodils are spring flowers. Can you name another flower that comes up in the spring?

Why is it hard to find Mr. Nibbles in the daffodils? What is camouflage?

15 - Is Mr. Nibbles disappointed?

17 - Do dogs dream? What is a dream? Do you dream?

18-20 – Have you seen the Moon in the sky? Could Mr. Nibbles reach the Moon? Could you reach the Moon?

21 - Do you take naps?

24 – What is Mr. Nibbles having for a snack?

* Contact your local animal shelter to find out more about adopting a pet.

*To find out more about the Moon go to the NASA (National Aeronautics and Space Administration) Website www.NASA.gov

Mr. Nibbles came from a local animal shelter to live with us. He loves to run outside, sleep, play ball and chase the Moon.

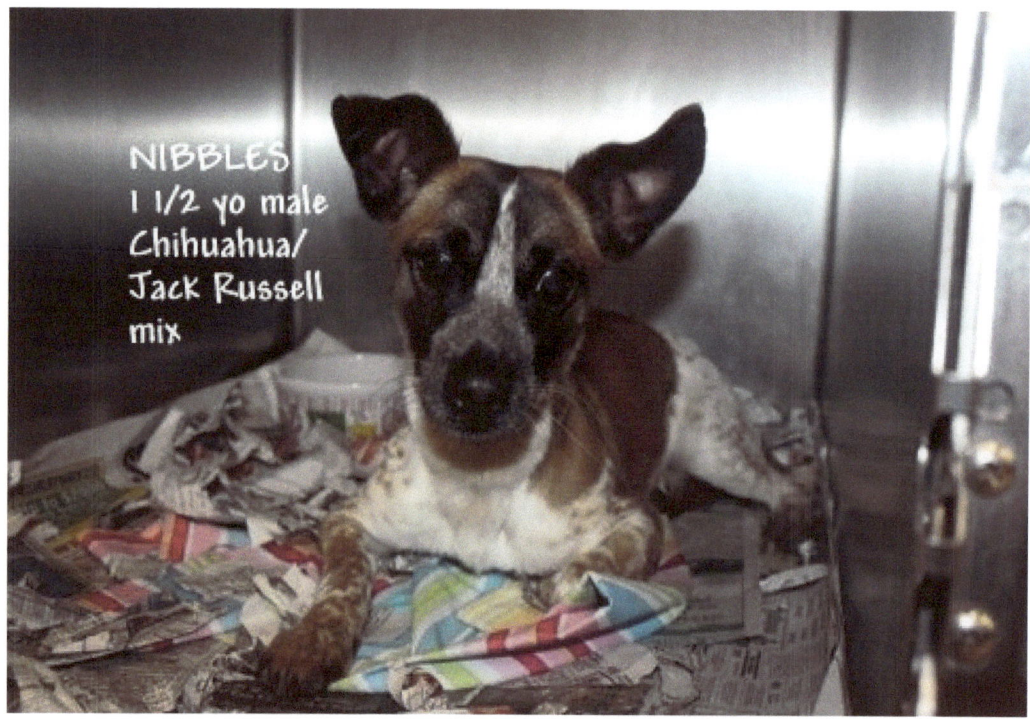

Looking for the Moon?

Mr. Nibbles sees the Moon everywhere. It is so tiny!

Can we go out to the yard and chase the Moon?

What happened to my Moon? Someone threw my Moon into the daffodils.

Can you follow Mr. Nibbles through the daffodils to find the Moon?

What does Mr. Nibbles have?

Wait a minute, that's not the Moon,

it's a squeaky ball!

But I had a dream that I jumped up and caught the Moon.

Sorry, Mr. Nibbles, it was only a dream.

But you did catch your squeaky ball.

This is the Moon at night.
It is very far away.

Sometimes you can see the Moon during the day.

All this Moon chasing makes me tired. I guess I'll take a nap.

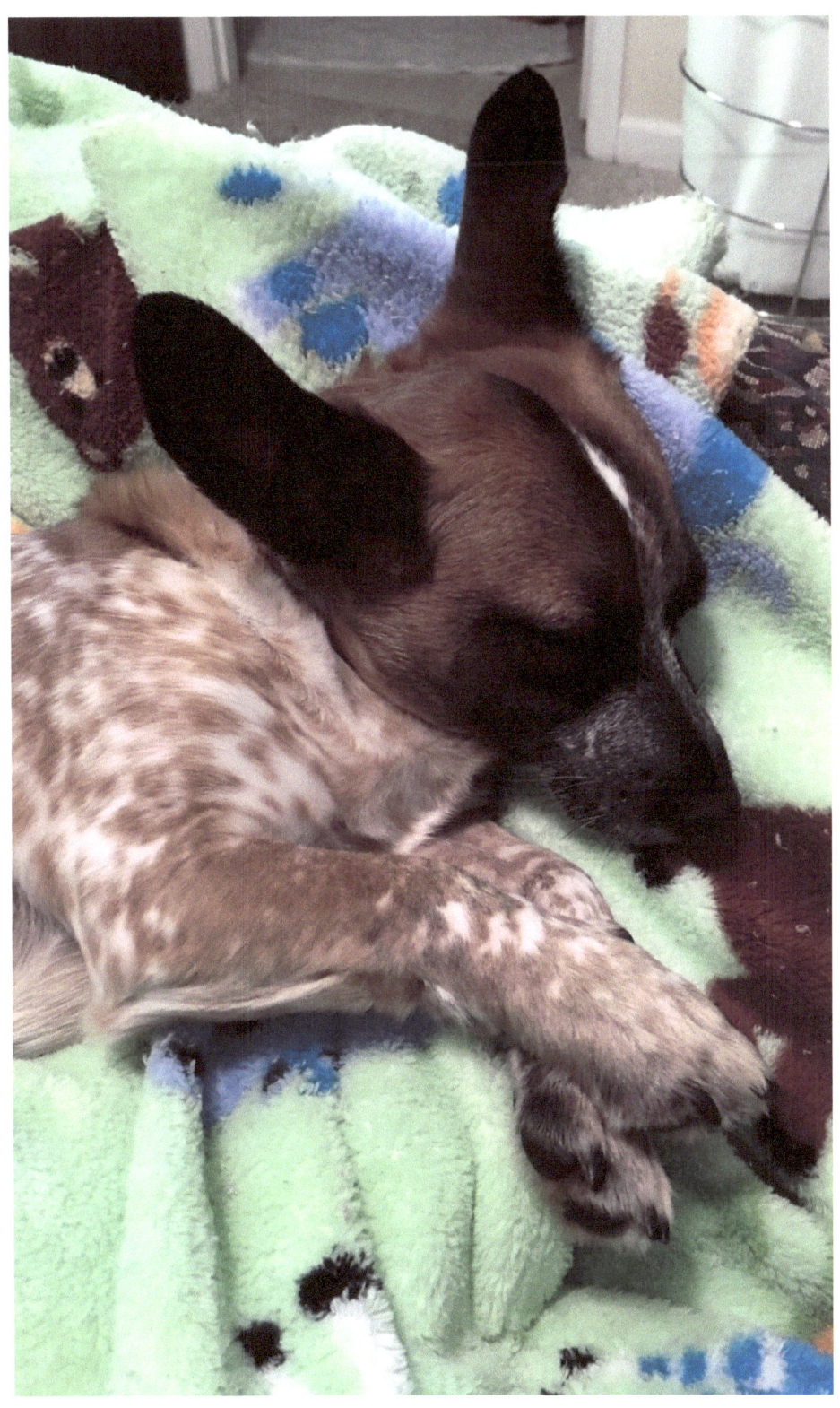

Up from his nap, Mr. Nibbles likes to have a snack before he goes out to play, again.

www.ingramcontent.com/pod-product-compliance
Lightning Source LLC
LaVergne TN
LVHW071030070426
835507LV00002B/95